This book is dedicated to my Dad, Mom, Elaine and Colleen — the best and loudest cheerleaders in heaven and on earth! Also, to Jason and my two boys, Connor and Jackson — thanks for making our home my favorite place in the world to be!

One day I woke up thinking
As I sometimes do
*"I wonder why people love me
And is it really true?"*

So I set out early that day
And had an awesome plan
I'd show them **I'm worth loving**
And make them understand

I brushed my teeth and **made my bed**
And even **did my chores**
I walked the dog and **fed my fish**
And headed out the door

I **did my best** all day at school
Got every question **right**
Ate all my lunch, played with new friends
And didn't even fight

I came home that day exhausted
It was **hard work being good**
I never knew if I made the grade
Though I did all that I could

I nodded off during supper
And Dad said he wanted to **talk**
So after we ate our potatoes and peas
We headed for our little walk

We walked right past my tidied room
And he smiled and looked at me
Then he took my hand and said: **"Come here
There is something I want you to see"**

He took me to his study
And I climbed upon his knee
And as I did he pointed to
A framed picture of me

It wasn't of me playing or reading
Or even kicking a ball
As a matter of fact I found it strange
I was doing nothing at all

My hair and clothes were messy
And I had a toothless grin
I even think I saw some **jam**
That landed on my chin

"It seems you had a busy day"
He said as he hugged me tight
"It must have been really hard
Trying to do **everything right.**"

"Don't think I do not notice
When you do your best and try
I just see you so exhausted
And kinda wondered why."

"I just wanted to make you love me"
I said as I sunk into his chest
"I just wanted to be *good enough*
So you wouldn't *love me less*"

"It may be hard to see," said Dad
"But my love is not for sale
How do you know you've done enough
If you succeed or if you fail ?"

I don't love you because of **what you do**
Whether you're **perfect** or **good** or **kind**
The reason that I love you

Is simply that you're mine

About the Illustrator

Korey Scott is an **illustrator** who specializes in **children's books**, **educational material**, and **funny** characters/cartoons.

He **loves his work** and tries to put something **unique** in each project while **learning something new** too. When he is not drawing (and many times when he is) you can find him telling jokes, making sound effects, speaking Spanish, and trying to **make people laugh.**

CPSIA information can be obtained at www.ICGtesting.com
Printed in the USA
LVIW01n1026100216
474425LV00007B/18